TABLE OF CONTENTS

OUR WORLD IN PICTURES

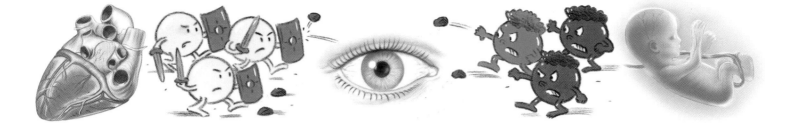

THE HUMAN BODY

AN INTRODUCTION FOR CHILDREN FROM 6 TO 10

Conception
Émilie BEAUMONT

Text
Agnès VANDEWIELE

Images
Milan illustrations agency
Giampietro COSTA
Mariano VALSESIA
C. HACHE

Translation
Lara M. ANDAHAZY

FLEURUS

THE BEGINNING OF LIFE

Men's and women's bodies are complementary—both are needed to produce a baby.

Every month women produce an "egg," or ovum, which waits to be fertilized by the sperm that men produce. At the same time, the woman's uterus gets ready to receive the baby-to-be. If the ovum is not fertilized, the uterus returns to normal and sheds the blood it was saving to nourish the baby. This is when the woman has her period.

When a man and woman love each other very much and want to have a baby, they unite their bodies and the man's sperm goes up into the woman's body to the fallopian tube where the ovum is waiting to be fertilized. A baby begins to grow if the sperm meets and fertilizes the egg.

BEFORE THE BABY IS BORN

A baby starts to develop when the ovum is fertilized. The father sends millions of spermatozoa to the uterus but only one enters the ovum. (There are two kinds of sperm and the baby will be a boy or girl depending on which kind fertilizes the egg.) At this point the fertilized ovum is a large cell inside a Fallopian tube that goes from the ovaries (which produce the ovum) to the uterus. The fertilized ovum divides in two after 36 hours and again into four after 48 hours, then into eight and so on until it is a group of about 100 cells.

This bunch of cells grows and descends into the uterus in about five days. There it will nest in a membrane pouch full of liquid. It is now an embryo which will continue to develop for 9 months before being born. It is linked to its mother by a sponge-like substance, the placenta, attached to the uterus and by an umbilical cord. The mother supplies the embryo with the oxygen and nutrients it needs to grow through the placenta and umbilical cord.

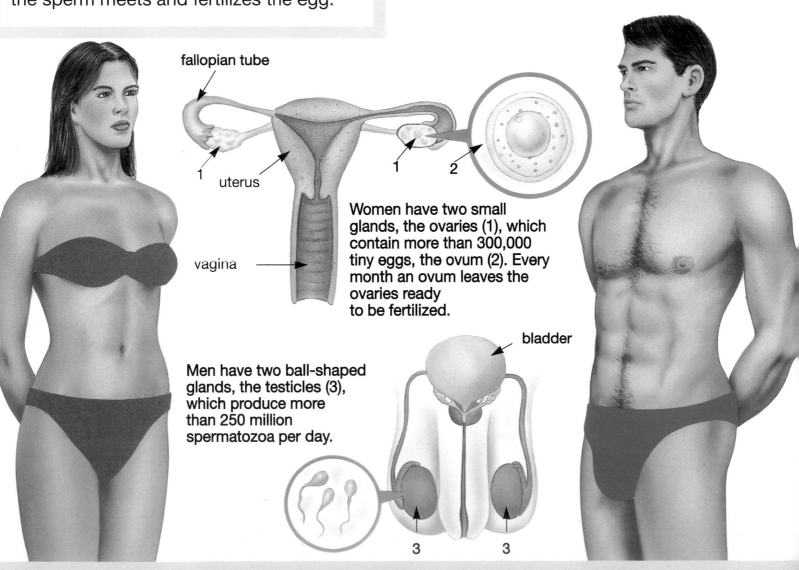

fallopian tube

1   uterus

vagina

1   2

Women have two small glands, the ovaries (1), which contain more than 300,000 tiny eggs, the ovum (2). Every month an ovum leaves the ovaries ready to be fertilized.

bladder

Men have two ball-shaped glands, the testicles (3), which produce more than 250 million spermatozoa per day.

3   3

The ovum is much larger than the spermatozoa.

A few hours after fertilization, the other sperm die. The fertilized ovum divides into two cells, then four and so on.

1

2

The small group of cells moves through the Fallopian tube (1) to the uterus (2) dividing and growing as it goes. It attaches itself to the uterus wall and continues to develop.

6 weeks

8 weeks

3 months

5 months

A BABY DEVELOPS

There are different stages of development in the uterus.
• When the embryo is 6 weeks old the head develops. This is the beginning of human shape.
• When it is 8 weeks old, the embryo is about an inch and a half long and weighs less than an ounce. The main body parts are there including fingers, toes and eyes.
• At 10 weeks old the embryo continues to grow and develop. It will soon look like a miniature baby.
• At 3 months old the growing baby is called a fetus. It is between three and five inches long and weighs just over an ounce. Its body is formed. It can open its mouth and swallow. Its genital organs start to develop. When the fetus is 4 months old we can see if it is a boy or a girl with an ultrasound scan.
• When the fetus is five months old it is about ten inches long and weighs just over one pound. It

has hair, eyelashes and eyebrows. Its kidneys and digestive system work. Sometimes it even sucks its thumb! Its mother can feel it move.
• After 9 months in the womb, the baby has grown a lot and weighs between 5 and 7 pounds. There is not a lot of space left in the uterus and the baby gets ready to be born. It will come out headfirst through its mother's vagina.

GROWING UP

As soon as we are conceived we start to grow. We continue to grow until we reach full size when we are about 18 or 20 years old. We learn a lot while we grow. First, we learn how to stand, walk and talk (at about two). During puberty, between 12 and 14 years old, boys' and girls' bodies change so that they will be able to have children one day. After that we go through two more stages: adulthood and old age.

The cells in the body are renewed throughout life. When we are old, our tissues get weaker, we get wrinkles and are more fragile.

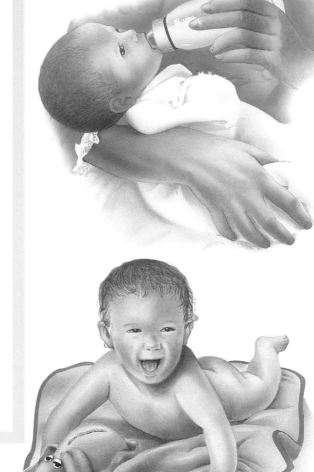

One-month-old babies drink milk. They start to smile but can't follow objects with their eyes yet. They gain about an ounce per day.

At two months old, babies lift their heads when they are placed on their stomachs. The baby in the picture to the left is using his arms to hold himself up. He is about 5 or 6 months old.

Five- or six-month-old babies grab objects with their hands and eat with spoons. They get their first teeth. They start to be able to sit for a long time and can stand up very well if we help them.

Seven- or eight-month-old babies like to play with blocks. They start to hold on to the bars on their cribs and try to stand up alone. They start to babble a few syllables.

Nine-month-olds can crawl. They babble a lot and repeat more and more syllables. They enjoy throwing objects to the ground.

One-year-olds start to walk. They are just over two feet tall and weigh about 20 pounds.

Six- and seven-year-olds play ball, dance, and participate in sports. They can do lots of things and like to play with their friends. They go to school where they learn to read, write and count.

Puberty
Between ten and sixteen, our bodies change. Girls grow pubic hair, their breasts develop and their hips get rounder. Their ovaries start to produce eggs and they will get their first period between 10 and 14 years old. Boys grow pubic hair, their shoulders get wider, their voices change, their penises get longer and their testicles start to produce sperm.

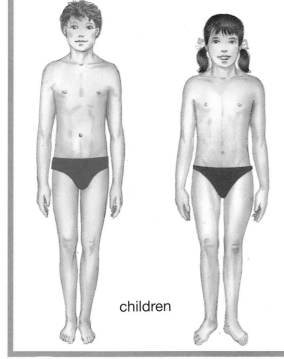

children

Not all parts of our bodies grow at the same speed. Babies' heads and bodies are much bigger in relation to their arms and legs than adults'. Later, our arms and legs grow much faster than our heads do.

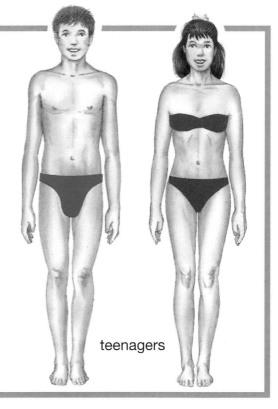

teenagers

Adults
Adulthood is the longest period of our lives. Many adults form families and have children. They become grandparents when their children grow up and have children of their own. Each set of children is a new generation.

TEETH AND NUTRITION

Our teeth let us eat the solid foods that helps us grow. Babies grow their first teeth between 6 and 8 months old. These first teeth are called baby or milk teeth. They are replaced later by our adult teeth. You use your teeth every time you eat to bite, chew and mash your food. The food gets mixed with saliva which makes it easy to digest and transformed to help you grow and give your body the energy it needs. Our bodies need varied food and about one and a half quarts of liquid every day to stay in good health.

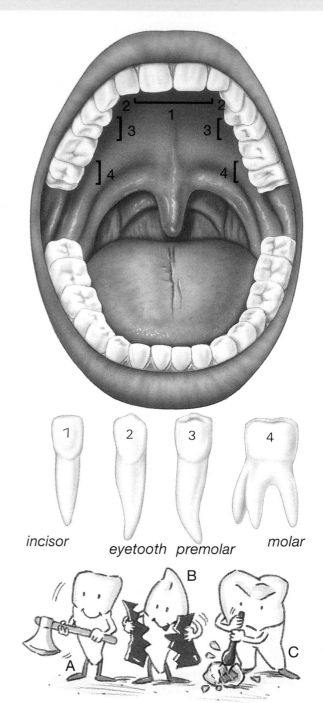

incisor   *eyetooth* *premolar*   *molar*

The Role of Teeth

Each of our teeth has a specific role. Incisors (A) cut food with their sharp edges. Eyeteeth (B) are the pointy teeth that tear food. Premolars and molars (C) have small bumps that grind up hard foods.

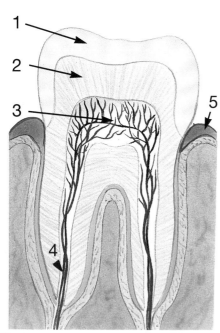

Teeth are covered with very hard enamel (1) that protects them from heat, cold and shocks. Underneath the enamel is the dentin (2) which is not as hard as the enamel. All the way inside is the pulp (3) in which tiny blood vessels and nerves are found (4). The pulp is the sensitive part. It reaches all the way down into the roots lodged in the gums (5).

Growing Brand-New Teeth!

When they are about two years old children have 20 milk teeth. Under each one is the beginnings of another tooth which helps the baby tooth fall out by destroying its roots. You loose all your baby teeth between 6 and 12 years old. Your adult teeth take their places. Adults have 32 teeth.

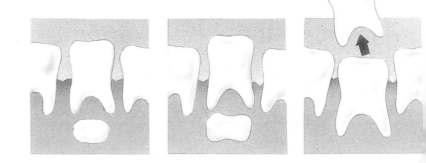

EATING

Our bodies are made up of billions of tiny cells that are constantly working, even when we are resting. We have to eat in order to give them energy and so that they can be replaced when they get old. Our bodies need lots of different foods.

If we eat too much or not enough our bodies do not function properly. Some people are hungry again right after eating. Some people eat way too much food all at once and then throw up; they suffer from bulemia. Others refuse to eat and loose too much weight; they suffer from anorexia.

If you eat too much and don't get enough exercise, too much fat builds up on your body and you can become obese. You need vitamin D to grow. It helps calcium attach itself to your bones. It is found in dairy products and liver. If you don't have enough vitamin D your bones stay fragile and don't grow. This is called rickets.

GET THE RIGHT FOODS!

We need to eat three or four meals a day. Our meals have to give us everything our cells need.

• Proteins help us build the cells in our muscles and organs. Proteins are found in meat, eggs, fish and cheese.

• Carbohydrates give us strength and energy. They are found in sugar, cereals, bread, rice and potatoes.

• Fats or lipids give us energy and protect us from the cold by forming a thin layer of fat under our skins. They are found in oil, butter, chocolate and nuts.

• Vitamins and minerals let you digest food properly and help in the creation of red blood cells and strengthen your muscles and bones. Fruits and vegetables contain lots of vitamins. Fish has lots of phosphorus (needed for memory) and calcium (that you need to grow).

 proteins

carbohydrates

fats

vitamins

MUSCLES AND BONES

Our muscles and bones make our bodies solid and let us move. Our skeletons are made up of 206 bones of different shapes. The spine supports the body. Other bones protect fragile organs: our skulls protect our brains and our ribs protect our lungs. The longest bone is the femur and the smallest is the stirrup bone in our ears. Muscles are supple and elastic. They cover our bones. We have about 650 different muscles. When they contract they pull on our bones and make our bodies move. They let us walk, run and jump.

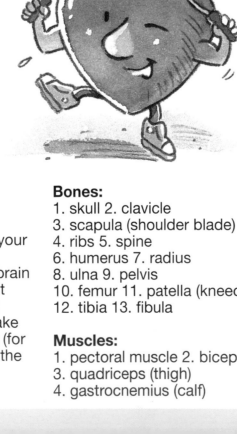

Muscles

Most muscles, like the ones in your arms, legs and hands, are voluntary. This means that the brain tells them when to contract. But some of your muscles contract automatically: your heart (to make your blood flow), your stomach (for digestion), and the muscles on the ribcage (to make you breathe). These are involuntary muscles.

Bones:
1. skull 2. clavicle
3. scapula (shoulder blade)
4. ribs 5. spine
6. humerus 7. radius
8. ulna 9. pelvis
10. femur 11. patella (kneecap)
12. tibia 13. fibula

Muscles:
1. pectoral muscle 2. biceps (arm)
3. quadriceps (thigh)
4. gastrocnemius (calf)

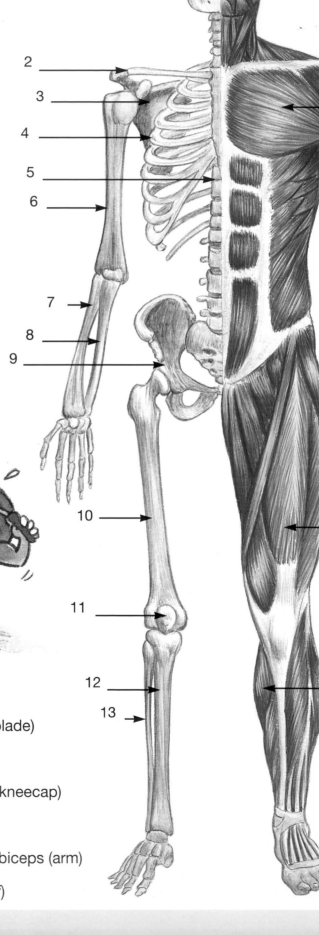

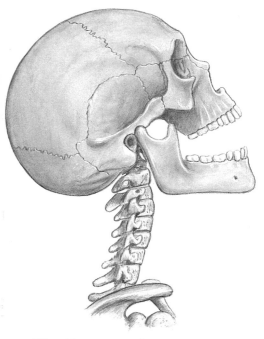

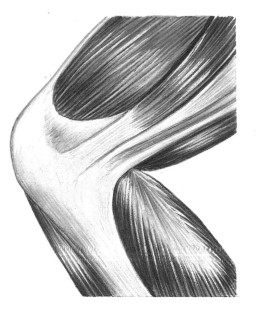

The Neck and Spine
Your head is carried by your spine. It is made up of 24 vertebrae hooked together. They let you bend and turn your head. The muscles in your neck make two vertebrae (the atlas and the axis) pivot against each other when you turn your head.

The Knees
They are the hinge joints between your thigh bones (the femur) and shin bones (tibia). When you bend your knees, the muscles on the

back of your thighs contract and pull on your tibias. A pocket of liquid, the synovia, between the bones in the knee joint lets them slide smoothly.

Are bones fragile?
No, they are solid but a violent jolt can break them. When you break an arm or a leg the doctor puts a plaster cast on you that keeps the broken bones from moving. The bones grow back together by themselves in a few weeks. If you pull too much on a ligament it stretches and sometimes breaks. This is what happens when you sprain your ankle.

What are goose bumps?
When you are cold, small muscles contract to make the hair on your skin stand up and close your pores to keep in the heat. They make goose bumps.

biceps

triceps

Bending and Straightening Your Arms
Your biceps and triceps are the muscles in front and in back of your arms. When you bend your arms, the biceps contract and pull on the bones in your forearm. At the same time your triceps stretch and your forearm moves up. When you straighten your arms the triceps contract and the

biceps stretch. Your forearm moves down. Your biceps and triceps are attached to your bones with tendons like all your muscles. Bones are linked by ligaments in your joints. The ends of your bones are covered by a smooth and elastic substance called cartilage that makes movement easier.

When do bones stop growing?
Children have extra cartilage at the ends of their bones. It hardens and makes their bones grow. When all the extra cartilage has hardened, the bones stop growing. This takes about 18 to 20 years. Crocodiles' bones never stop growing!

13

THE BRAIN

Your brain is what controls everything that your body does. Everything your body feels reaches the brain by your nerves. Your brain sorts them, decodes them and orders the necessary reactions. Your brain is made up of three parts: the cerebral trunk or mainstem (A) makes you breathe, your heart beat and your blood circulate even when you sleep; the cerebellum (B) coordinates your movements; and the cortex (C). The surface of your cortex is covered with millions of wrinkles and is divided into different sections. Each area controls something different like feeling, speaking, writing, moving and remembering (see the big picture in the center).

THE NERVOUS SYSTEM

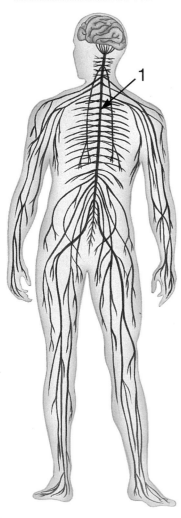

This is the big communication system that connects your brain to the rest of your body. The spinal cord (1) is the central axis. It starts at the base of the brain and follows the spine. It branches out into thousands of nerves that reach every part of your body. If you burn your hand your nerves send a message to your brain and your brain tells your hand to move. If your spinal cord is damaged by a serious accident it can no longer send the messages and you can be paralyzed.

The Hypothalamus (4) regulates feelings of hunger, thirst, temperature, fear and anger.

The Visual Zone (1) interprets the messages sent by your eyes.
▼

The Cerebellum (B) coordinates your body's movements and helps you keep your balance.
▼

7

3

1

The Language Zone (3) ▶
decodes what you read and hear. A different area controls your lips and vocal cords.

The Medulla (5) ▶
is inside the cerebral mainstem. It controls your heartbeat and breathing even when you sleep.

◀ **The Taste Zone (7)**
lets you recognize different flavors (sugar, salt, etc.) in the foods you eat.

The Motor Zone (6)
controls the movements of your voluntary muscles. ▼

C

6

3'

2

8

4

A

5

▲
The Auditory Zone (2)
interprets and recognizes the sounds you hear.

◀ **Memory**
is controlled by two areas of the brain. One records old memories and the other new memories. But we don't know exactly which yet because memory is a very complicated process.

The Odor Zone (8) ▶
lets you recognize smells.

THE CIRCULATORY SYSTEM

Your blood moves continuously throughout your whole body from your head to your feet. It brings all your muscles and vital organs (liver, stomach, lungs, etc.) the energy they need. Your heart beats night and day and never stops; it is the motor that moves your blood. This surprising muscle the size of your fist works on its own. You have 3 quarts of blood (adults have 5) in your body and your heart pushes it through countless small and large blood vessels. If you put all your blood vessels end to end they would stretch several thousand miles! Your blood moves at different speeds depending on how fast or slow your heart beats.

BLOOD

Blood is made up of several kinds of tiny cells or corpuscles floating in a liquid called plasma. The different cells are:
• Red blood cells (1). They give blood its color and carry oxygen to the lungs and other organs.
• White corpuscles (2). They help keep us from getting sick. They multiply and fight off germs that enter our bodies.
• Platelets (3). They make our blood coagulate when we cut ourselves. They form a clot that stops the bleeding. Hemophiliacs' blood doesn't coagulate properly.

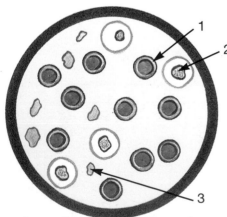

a drop of blood seen through a microscope

an imaginary battle between a germ and white corpuscles

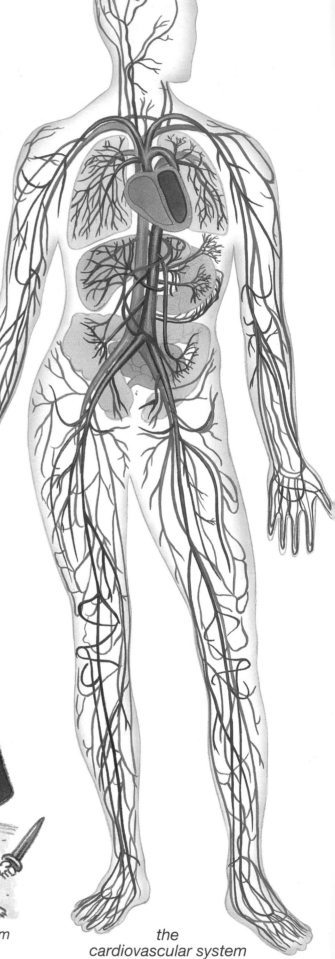

the cardiovascular system

16

CIRCULATION

In order to irrigate your whole body your blood leaves the heart by your arteries. It gives oxygen to all your muscles and organs. It is cleaned when it goes through your liver and kidneys and picks up nutrition in the intestine. Then it is carried back to the heart by veins and takes the muscles' and tissues' waste (carbon dioxide) with it. We call this part systemic circulation. It is the big loop in a figure eight shaped path (your heart is in the middle). From your heart, the blood carries the waste to your lungs. There it gets rid of the waste and picks up fresh oxygen which it takes back to the heart. This part is called pulmonary circulation.

An adult heart is the size of a closed fist and weighs between 9 and 11 ounces. It is a surprising machine designed to beat for 80 to 100 years or more non-stop.

THE HEART

The heart is a hollow muscle divided into four chambers: two auricles on top and two ventricles on the bottom. The heart acts like a pump. To make your blood move it pulls in blood by dilating (opening wider) and pushes it out by contracting (squeezing). When it contracts, your blood is pushed out of the left ventricle towards the rest of your body. It comes back into the right auricle when it dilates. When the hearts contracts again your blood moves into the right

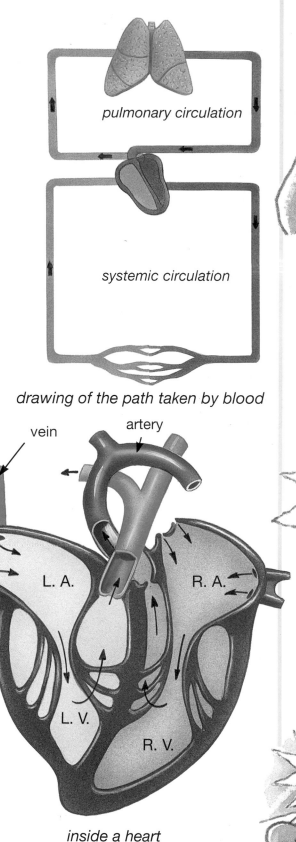

pulmonary circulation

systemic circulation

drawing of the path taken by blood

vein   artery

L. A.   R. A.

L. V.

R. V.

inside a heart

ventricle and then towards your lungs. Then it returns to fill the left auricle when it dilates and so on. Your heart dilates and then contracts 70 times per minute. This is your heartbeat.

What does the doctor do?
He listens to your heartbeat with his stethoscope. He can hear the noise made by the valves that act like doors between the auricles and ventricles. They open and close each time your heart beats to let your blood through.

What is a heart attack?
Your heart is fed by small arteries (called coronary arteries) like all your muscles. If a blood clot blocks them your heart doesn't work properly and can even stop. This is called a coronary or a heart attack.

Can you change hearts?
We now know how to replace hearts that are very damaged by transplanting new ones. Replacements come from organ donors, people who are willing to give their organs if they die in an accident.

17

SPEECH AND BREATHING

We breathe in order to get the oxygen we need to live. Our respiratory system is made up of two lungs. Air goes in your nose and mouth and enters your lungs through tubes that get smaller and smaller as they go. It's like an upside-down tree: the trunk is the windpipe, the large branches are the bronchial tubes and the leaves are the air cells or alveoli. Your blood gets oxygen and gets rid of carbon dioxide in the alveoli. Breathing also lets us talk because we make sounds and words by making the air vibrate in our throats and mouths.

The Respiratory System

Your lungs work like an air pump that is moved by the muscles on your ribcage. They make them fill up and empty out like a balloon. When you breathe in air goes from your nose and mouth to the windpipe or trachea (1) and enters both lungs through your bronchial tubes (2). They divide into smaller bronchioles (3) that take the air to the alveoli. Your lungs are made up of millions of these tiny sac-like air cells. Air is filtered in the alveoli and oxygen moves into tiny blood vessels called capillaries. Your blood takes the oxygen and sends carbon dioxide into your lungs. Your get rid of the carbon dioxide when you breathe out. The movements you make to breathe are involuntary. You do it without thinking about it. But when you want to you can breathe in and out faster or slower. You can even hold your breath for a little while.

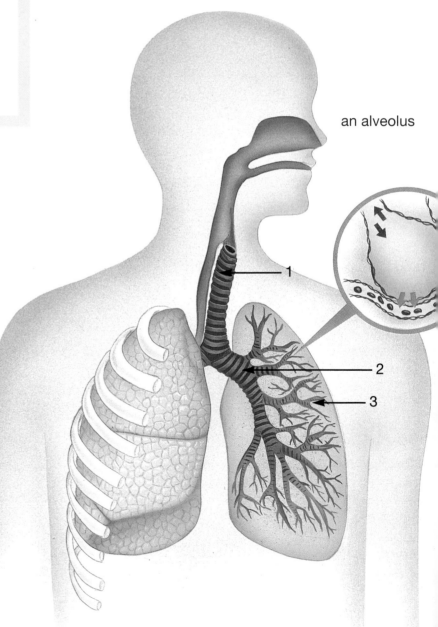

an alveolus

1

2

3

Breathing In and Out

When you breathe in (A), the muscles on your ribcage lift up your ribs. Your diaphragm (the muscle under your ribs) lowers.
The volume of your ribcage gets bigger and air is pulled in by your lungs as they fill up.
When you breathe out (B), your muscles relax, your ribs go down and your lungs get smaller. Air is pushed out.

A   B

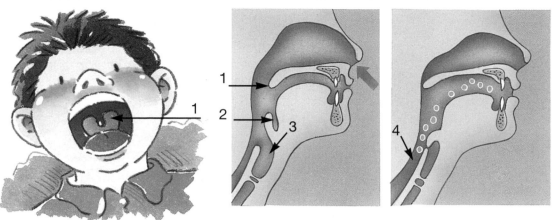

What does the uvula do?

The uvula (1) and the epiglottis (2) are two small doors at the back of the mouth. They open to let air coming in through the nose and mouth into the lungs by way of the trachea (3). They close when we eat so that food goes into the esophagus (4) and not the lungs.

Do we take in lots of air?
One-year-olds breathe about 30 times a minute and inhale more than two quarts of air. Adults breathe 14 times a minute and inhale 7 quarts of air.

Where do our voices come from?

The larynx produces the sounds you make. It is like a small music box in your throat across which your vocal cords are stretched. The air coming out of your lungs makes them vibrate. When the cords are close together the sound is high pitched. When they are apart the sound is deep.

What causes hiccups?
Hiccups are caused when the diaphragm contracts sharply. This is sometimes caused by swallowing too quickly. Even babies get the hiccups.

A. Vocal cords are far apart when you breathe.

B. They move close together when you speak.

A

B

Why do we have to catch our breath when we run?
When we run we need more energy and use more oxygen. To get the oxygen we need we take lots of quick breaths closer together.

Boys' voices change.

When boys are about 14 years old their throat and mouth muscles develop and the Adam's apple (1) appears. This makes their voices change and get deeper.

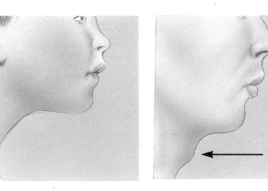

Cigarettes are bad for you.
Cigarettes contain dangerous chemicals that get into your lungs when you smoke. They damage your lungs and can cause very serious diseases like cancer.

THE DIGESTIVE SYSTEM

The human body needs energy to maintain its cells which work constantly. But the body can not use the energy in food directly. It needs to transform the food you eat. This is the digestive system's job. It is basically a tube that goes from your mouth to your anus. Food follows this tube and is reduced to a thin gruel by gastric juices. The nutrition contained in the food can then enter the blood stream which carries it to all the cells in the body. The nutrients are absorbed. This voyage through the digestive tract takes about 30 hours.

The digestive system's job

The digestive system transforms food into tiny particles so that they can be absorbed by the blood stream. This way all the cells in your body can be fed.

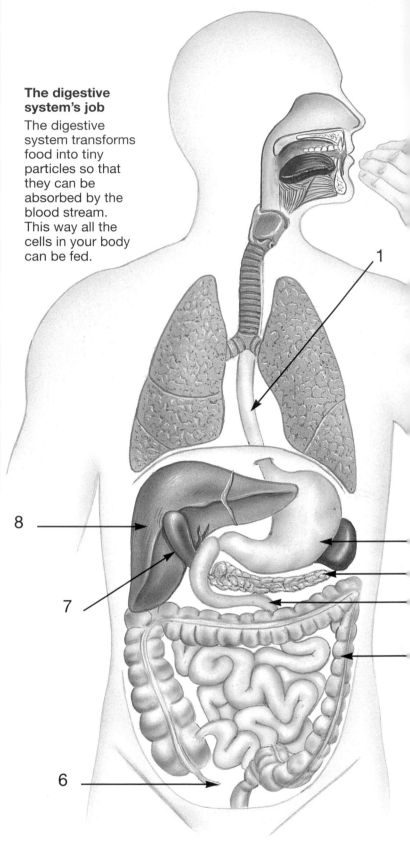

When kidneys stop working

If one kidney doesn't work, the other does its work for it. If both stop working a dialysis machine, or artificial kidney, can be used to help the patient (see the picture above). The patient's blood is sent through the machine which cleans it for the kidneys.

THE DIGESTIVE SYSTEM

The digestive tract starts at the mouth and goes to the stomach, then the intestines. Food is transformed little by little as it moves along. In the mouth, your teeth chew the food and saliva softens it, turning it into a small lump, the bolus, which goes down the esophagus into the stomach.

Then the stomach mixes the bolus with the gastric juices it produces and reduces it to a fine gruel (meals rest from 2 to 4 hours in the stomach). The gruel then moves on into the small intestine where it meets other gastric juices produced by the liver (bile) and the pancreas. They help complete digestion. The intestinal walls filter the gruel and the nutritious elements move into the bloodstream. A vein carries them to the liver which changes them into energy which is delivered to the whole body by the blood. The useless elements move into the large intestine and are then ejected by the anus in the form of stools.

THE URINARY SYSTEM

Our bodies need lots of water. The water in the bloodstream continually needs to be purified and renewed (60 times a day). The urinary system, with two kidneys, does this job. Kidneys are two bean-shaped organs the size of a fist made up of millions of tiny filters.

—2

3

—4

5

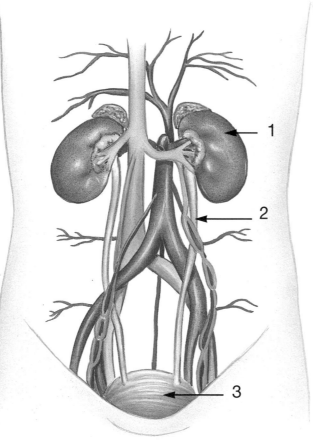

The waste produced by the cells and dissolved in the bloodstream are carried to the kidneys by the renal arteries. There, the dirty blood is cleaned and 80% of the clean water returns to the blood. The rest goes the the bladder via two tubes, urethras, and is evacuated by another urethra in the form of urine.

If you eat too much or if you eat something that has gone bad your stomach (a muscle) reacts. Both it and your diaphragm contract to get rid of what's bad. This contraction makes you vomit.

If you have an infection inside your intestines the food does not stay in them long enough. It is still liquid when it comes out. This is called diarrhea. If you don't eat enough fruits and vegetables, or if you don't get enough exercise, the large intestine moves slower. The undigested food stays inside too long and gets hard. This is called constipation.

The appendix is a tiny open sack on the large intestine. It can get infected when something gets stuck in it. This inflammation is called appendicitis. You feel a very sharp pain in your lower right stomach. Infected appendixes need to be removed by a very simple operation.

21

THE FIVE SENSES

The five senses are sight, hearing, smell, touch and taste. We have special organs for each sense: eyes for sight, ears for hearing, the nose for smell, hands and fingers for touch and the tongue for taste. These organs receive sensations that they send to the brain through nerves. The brain decodes these sensations. It is really the brain that sees images, hears sounds, distinguishes colors and tastes food. Your five senses and your brain let you discover the world around you. You can see the wonders of nature, smell different things, hear sounds and taste food.

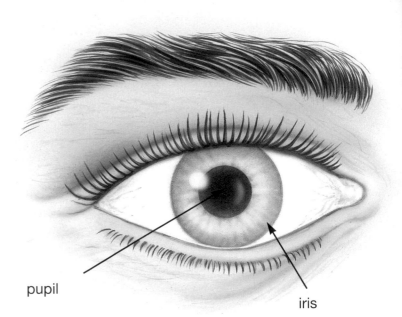

pupil

iris

When you look at an eye you can see a colored ring in the middle, the iris (1). In the very center is a black spot, the pupil (2). Light enters your eyes through the pupil. It crosses the crystalline lens (3) and projects images on a small screen, the retina (4), at the very back of your eye. The optic nerve (5) sends the image to the brain.

In order to project a clear image on the retina, the lens changes shape depending on if you are looking at an object close by or far away. But if your eye isn't perfect, the image is fuzzy. If you have trouble seeing far you are near-sighted. When you get old the lens gets harder and close objects look fuzzy. Eye glasses or contact lenses can fix this.

Your pupil changes shape. When there is a lot of light entering the eye the pupil gets smaller to keep some out. When there is not a lot of light it gets bigger to let more in.

SIGHT

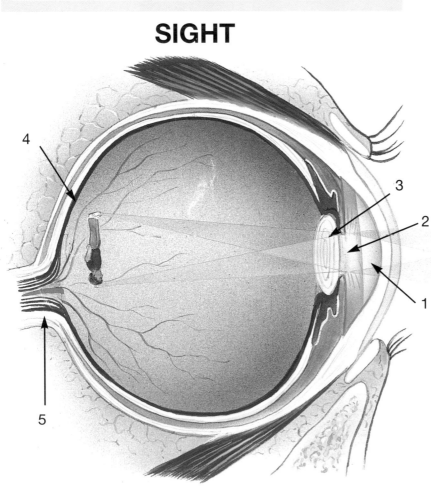

Why do we have two eyes?

When you look at an object with both eyes two upside down images are projected onto your retinas. Your brain turns them right side up and makes one image out of them. You have a wider field of vision with two eyes than with just one. You can see the difference when you close one eye. When you blink or cry lacrimal fluid (your tears) wets your eyes and gets rid of dust. You blink more that 5,000 times per day!

HEARING

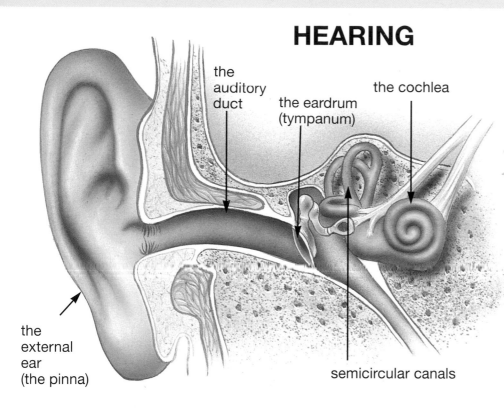

the auditory duct

the eardrum (tympanum)

the cochlea

the external ear (the pinna)

semicircular canals

Very loud sounds are dangerous. The vibrations they cause can damage the eardrum or the nerves in the ear and make you deaf. You need to protect your ears.

Ears

Your ears are the organs that let you hear and keep your balance. When sounds reach the ear they are collected by the pinna or external ear. They go through the auditory duct to a membrane called the tympanum—your eardrum. They make it vibrate. A chain of three little bones transmits the vibrations to a liquid inside a spiral-shaped canal called the cochlea. Nerves take the signals to the brain from here. The brain "hears" the sounds and interprets them as noise, words or music.

We can see colors because of special cells on the retina. If you don't have enough you have trouble telling colors like green and red apart. This is called being colorblind.

Balance

In your inner ear are three rings called semicircular canals next to the cochlea. They control our balance. They are full of liquid that moves a little bit when we move a lot. These signals are taken to the brain by nerves so that the brain knows what position we are in. The brain can then give orders to the body so you can catch your balance. When you are on a boat tossed about by lots of waves this liquid moves too much and you loose your sense of balance. Some people get seasick when this happens. The same thing can happen in cars on twisty roads.

This little boy can keep his balance standing on a ball thanks to his internal ear.

Vampires in horror films have red eyes to scare their victims. But if your eyes are red you have an infection or you looked directly at the sun. You need to see a doctor when your eyes are red.

TASTE

Your tongue lets you taste things that are good or bad. It is covered with thousands of tiny taste buds called papillae that pick up flavors. The taste buds on the tip of your tongue taste sweet or salty things. The ones on the sides of your tongue taste sour things like lemons. The ones at the back of your tongue taste bitter things like onions or orange peels. Saliva mixes with your food because the taste buds work best on liquids. Your tongue can also feel hot, cold and pain. Nerves carry all these feelings to the brain which "recognizes" them.

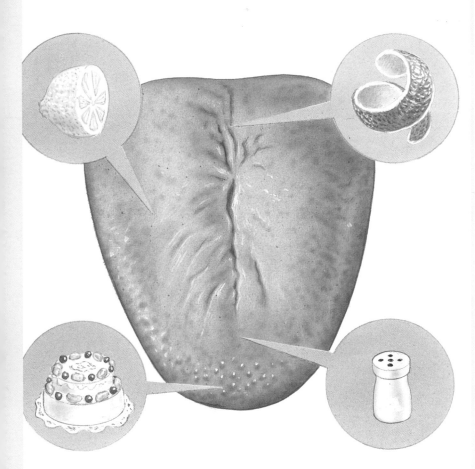

You don't only taste with your tongue. Your nose helps too. Very tiny bits of food get into your nose which "smells" their taste. When you have a cold your nose is plugged and food has less taste. When food has gone bad your nose and mouth tell the brain so you can spit it out. You and your friends can have fun recognizing food blindfolded!

SMELL

Inside your nose on top there are olfactory receptors (1) made of fuzzy cells called cilia that detect odors. When tiny particles carried by air touch them they send messages to the brain that "recognizes" them. Your sense of smell tells you if something is good or bad. The good smell of a cake can make you want to eat it. If fish smells bad you don't want to. The smell of gas warns you of danger. Your sense of smell depends on how many olfactory receptors you have in your nose. Dogs have a lot more than we do so their sense of smell is much better.

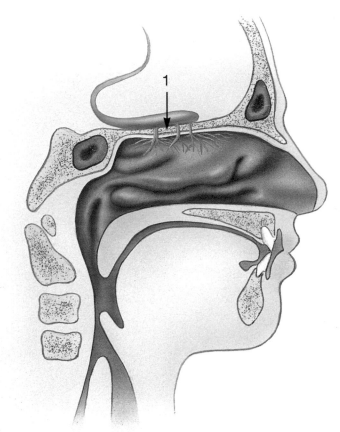

People who invent perfumes are called "noses" because their sense of smell is very good. A good "nose" can identify up to 3,000 smells.

TOUCH

Your fingers and skin let you feel the shape of objects and whether they are hot or cold and hard or soft. Your skin can also feel pain, like when you get hit. Your skin has thousands of nerve endings that send these messages to the brain. Our bodies are more sensitive in some areas than in others because they have more nerve endings. Your eyes, lips, face and hands are very sensitive.

SKIN

Your skin is the organ for the sense of touch. It also protects you from germs and helps the body adjust to hot or cold temperatures. When it is hot we sweat and when our sweat evaporates we cool down. When it is cold our pores close up to keep in heat. Our skin is about one eighth of an inch thick and is made up of two layers of cells: the epidermis and the dermis. The surface of your skin is renewed every 3 to 4 weeks. The dermis contains the muscles, sweat glands, tiny blood vessels that feed the skin and thousands of nerve endings that "feel" things.

The numerous nerve endings in your fingers are very close together and let you feel things in a lot of detail. Your brain interprets the many messages and can "feel" that cats have soft fur.

When you touch a sharp, pointy or hot object your brain gives the order to take your hand away.

The inside of your skin:
1. epidermis
2. dermis
3. sudorific or sweat gland
4. hair muscle
5. hair

When the sun is very strong you can get a sunburn or sunstroke. Your skin tans to protect you. But too much sun makes it red to warn you to get out of the sun and protect your skin with suntan lotion.

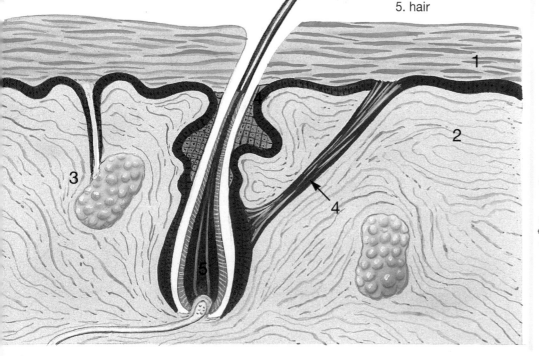

The color of your skin is caused by melanin. The more you have, the darker your skin. People from hot, sunny countries tend to have a lot. Their dark skin protects them from the sun better.

TAKING CARE OF YOUR BODY

Your body is a wonderful machine able to do thousands of different things like running, listening, talking and thinking and so on. You need to take good care of your body by keeping it clean so that germs don't make you sick, eating right and getting enough sleep. Exercise makes your heart, lungs and muscles work and makes your body stronger. Sometimes the different mechanisms in your body stop working as well as usual and you get sick. Doctors can make you better and sometimes you might need to go to the hospital.

GET ENOUGH EXERCISE

You need exercise every day to stay healthy and in good shape. Moving your body helps your blood circulate, makes you breathe deeply and maintains and develops your muscles. Lots of organs work to give you the energy you need. If you don't get enough exercise your body and muscles get weaker.

STAY CLEAN

Washing every day with soap and water gets rid of the dust, dirt and sweat that can block your pores and prevent your skin from breathing. You also have to wash your hair regularly with shampoo. Your hair protects your head from the sun and the cold. Don't forget to brush your teeth after every meal. If you do forget, tiny bits of food get stuck to your teeth and can cause cavities.

VISIT THE DOCTOR

Sometimes germs attack our bodies. Some, like viruses for example, cause contagious diseases like the flu, rubella or mumps. Your body reacts and you get a fever. Your white blood cells make antibodies that destroy the germs. The doctor examines your throat, listens to your breathing and prescribes medicine to make you better. He can also vaccinate you so you don't catch certain diseases.

SLEEP

Your body rests while you sleep but it doesn't shut down. It works at a different pace. It grows, your organs (such as the heart and stomach) continue to work and any cuts or scrapes you got during the day heal. There are three different phases of sleep: light sleep, deep sleep, and a period during which we dream. We spend about one third of our lives asleep. Children need more sleep than adults do because their bodies need more rest in order to grow. Babies need about 19 hours of sleep, 8-year-olds need at least 11 hours and adults need about 8 hours.

ISBN 2-215-06164-2